My Louisiana Life: Adult Colo
Adult Coloring Book Containi
and Memories
Author: Natalie Butler

MW01283290

Printed by CreateSpace

Copyright Natalie Butler, 2017

Printed in the United States.

ISBN-13:978-1979095433
ISBN-101979095434

I recommend using colored pencils in this book due to the paper quality. The use of markers could lead to ink bleeding through the paper.

Enjoy your coloring book tour of Louisiana!
Recreational therapists, activity therapists, teachers, etc. feel free to copy and use for your classworks/therapy/art sessions.

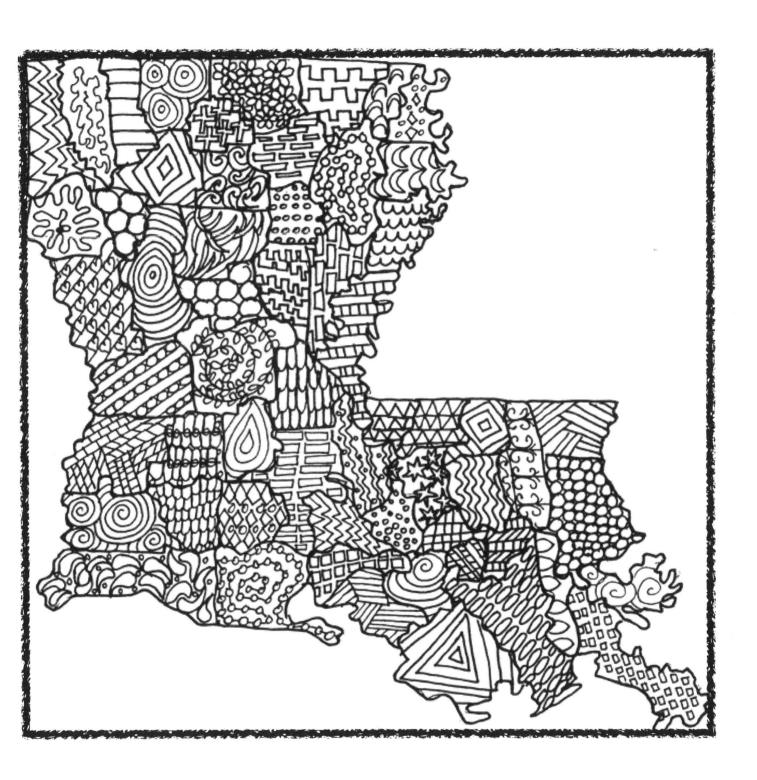

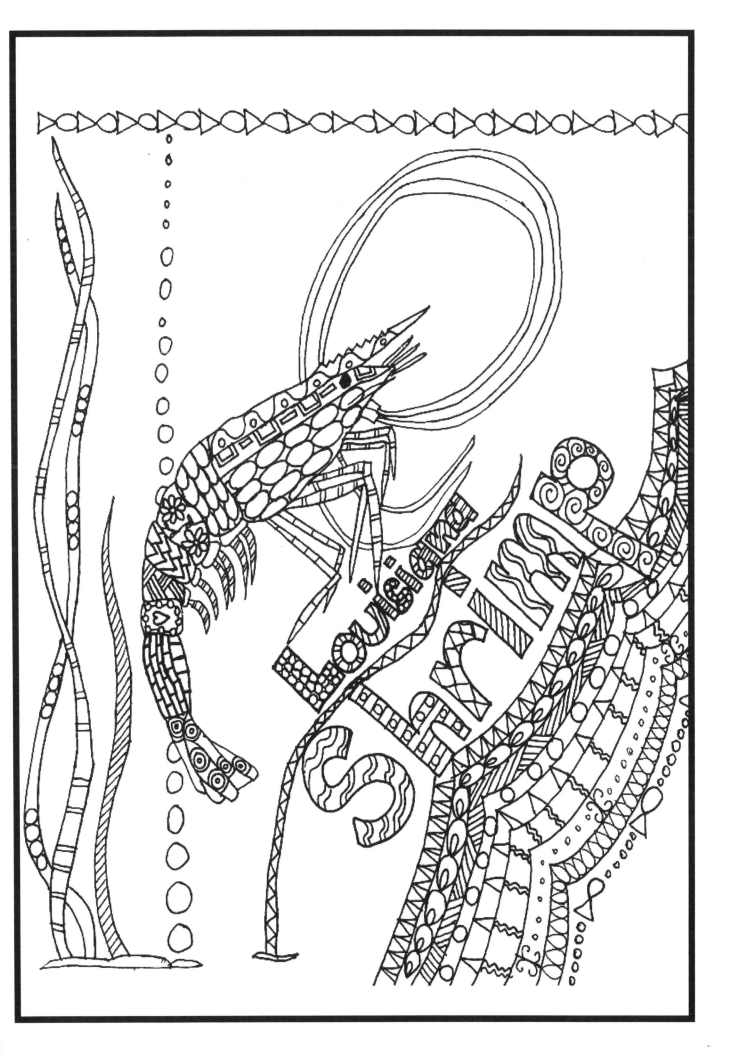

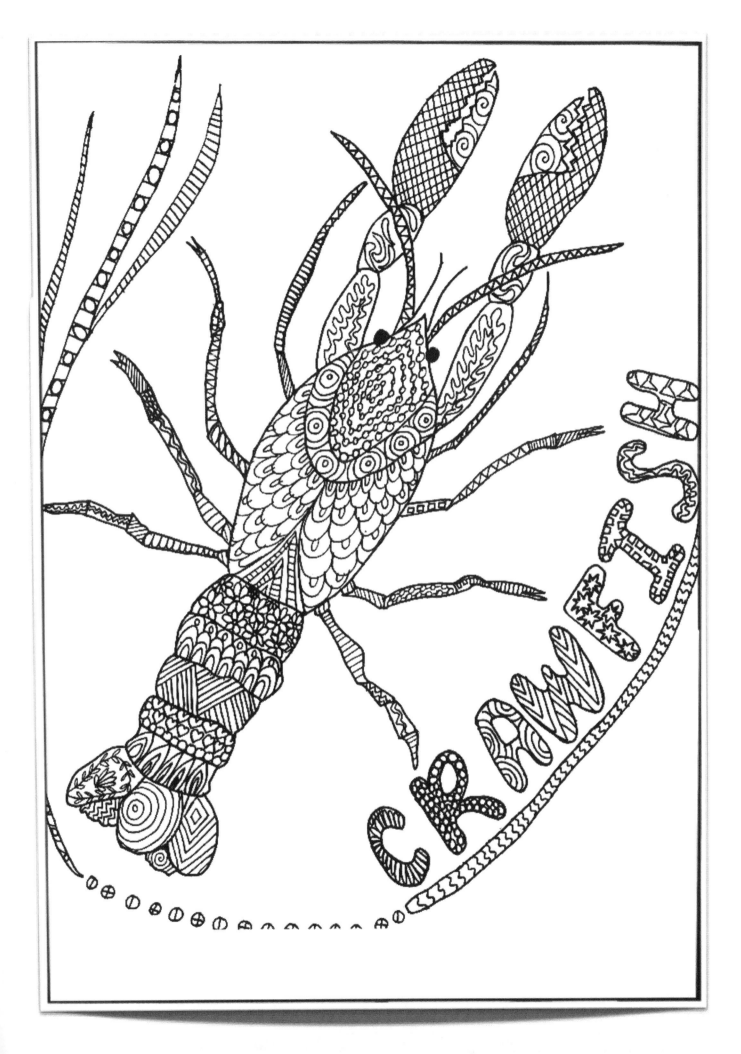

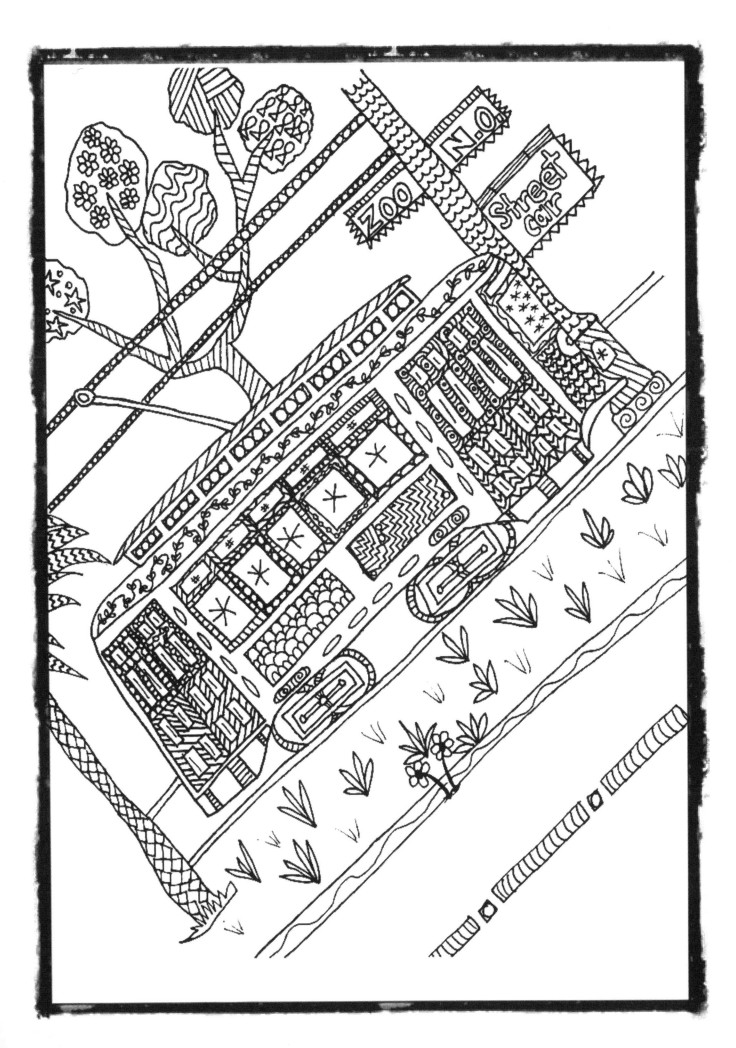

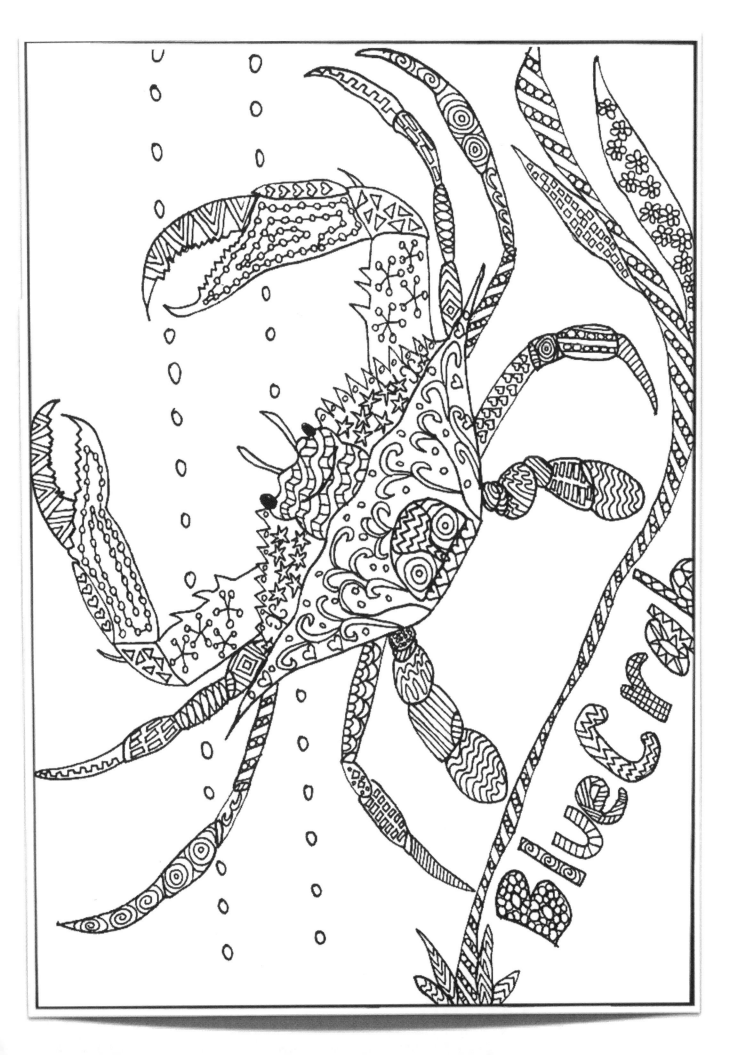

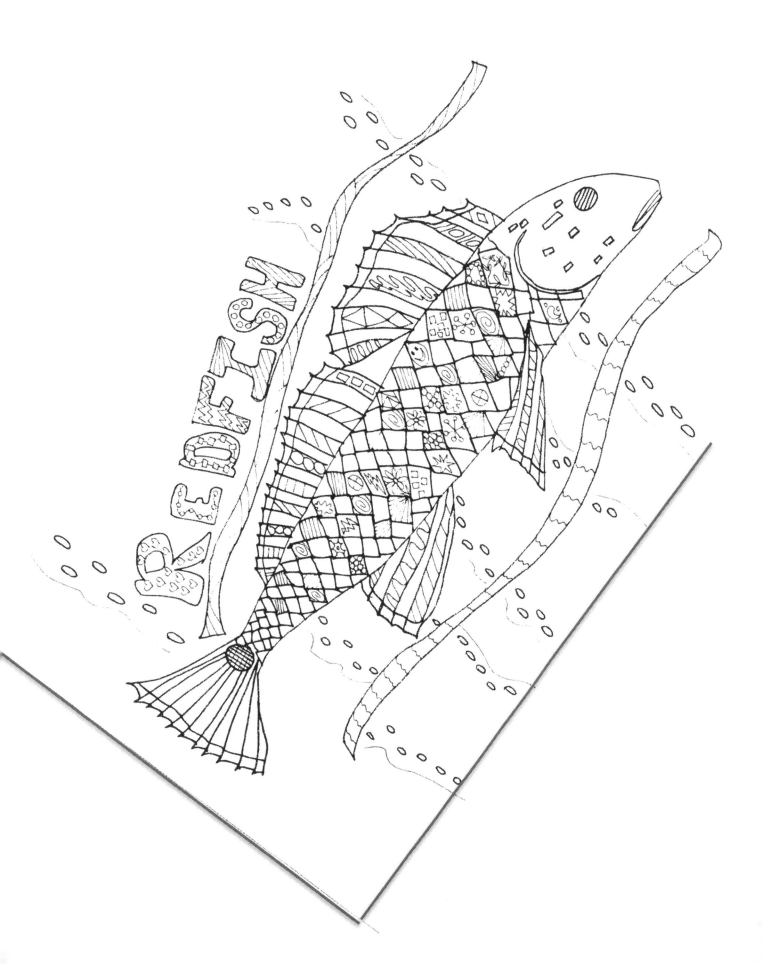

Made in the USA
Columbia, SC
24 June 2024

37171224R00017